I L(

WHEN...

BY SALLY FRANZ
ILLUSTRATED BY PETER STANDLEY

Nightingale Press

an imprint of Wimbledon Publishing Company Ltd.

LONDON

ISBN: 1903222 37 0

Produced in Great Britain
Printed and bound in Hungary

...when he is an hour late and calls
me from a bar. He always means to say,
'I'm sorry, I miss you, my friends are jerks.
I'm going to leave them and come home to you
as soon as I can without hurting their feelings.
I love you!' What he actually says is, 'Yeah,
right, it's me, running late, get there
when I can. Yeah, me too!'

...when he takes charge of the world, especially at pedestrian crossings when he punches the button for the light to change over and over again until it obeys him. He does it in lifts as well. My hero.

...when he helps me around the house when I get sick. He's so creative: cards, breakfast in bed. And clever! He put the laundry, dirty dishes and frozen dinner into the dishwasher and got all the housework done at once. Now, I wonder where the dog has gone? He needed a bath.

...when he is generous and giving. Why, just last week he got completely trashed and bought a round of drinks for everyone in his favorite sports bar...with the rent money.

...when he is a good father.
He spends all his weekends, holidays and two
evenings a week with the children from his
first marriage. I don't mind, it's just that after
three years of marriage I had hoped to have
met them by now.

...when I come home late and all
the lights are out. I can always tell if
he's home because the trail of dirty clothes
leads me towards the sounds of snoring,
belching and grunting coming from his TV
chair. It's like stalking a big, furry
hibernating bear in sweat socks.

...when he calls me in the middle of the day. Especially if I am screening my calls and my pager is on vibrate mode! This is the closest to foreplay we've got in six years.

...when he kisses me good night, holds me in his arms and sings to me. If you asked him he couldn't tell you what colour my eyes are, but never mind. He always finds his way home to the right house and that's enough for me!

...when he is a Master of
the Universe. A fax, a phone,
e-mail, scanner, mini-printer, voice-mail
pager and a CD player with headphones, all
dangling jauntily from his leather belt. Of
course it's a bit intimidating, when making
love, to know my every word could be
transmitted into 38 million homes if my
elbow hits the wrong button.

...when he rearranges the furniture and refuses my help. He's in the living room lifting, pulling and hoisting as if he were twenty again. Then he disappears into the den and rolls around on the floor in muscle spasms, holding his sides and groaning about a possible hernia for the rest of the day.

...when he helps with the baby.
He is so tender and kind and I know the baby
doesn't mind if sometimes at two a.m. he puts
the nappy on the wrong end.

...when he promised to take care of his past baggage. So he invited his ex-wife on holiday. I'm as open-minded as the next woman, but I still don't think we should have to share our king-size bed with her!

...when he gets all cleaned up for a night out. Then he leaves the wet towels on the bedroom carpet. But it's turned out great - I've been able to take the damp parts and start a small mushroom farm. The extra cash has come in quite handy.

...when he decides to save us money. After all, real men can build things from kits. In fact, he is still in the garden putting together the *J.R. Hewing Southfork Outdoor Grill Kit # 386* that he bought in 1979. Every year we get a little closer to a real American barbecue.

...when he's all manly and macho!
He loves to watch violent videos, wrestling,
hockey, car racing, and old war films.
Of course, when I had the baby he wouldn't
come in to the delivery room and watch the
birth. He said he couldn't stand the
sight of blood.

...when he surprises me with company for dinner. Thanks to him I even won an award at the fair this year for my recipe: Hungarian stew for forty from two pork chops and one large baked potato.

...when we are in the car,
miles from the nearest village, and
he reassures me that he knows where he
is. Very well, dear, somewhere between the
two coasts, the core of the earth and the sun.
But now, Aunt Hildy's house has gone missing.
So, what say we ask that nice man at the
petrol station we have already passed six
times if he has a clue where they've
moved her house.

...when he dresses himself in stripes and tartan. I wonder if the wife of a circus clown has the same problem, but in reverse: 'Just where do you think you're going in that three-piece suit and Thomas Pink shirt and tie? I will not have you coming to Sunday dinner at my mum's looking like a banker. Where is the lovely pink shirt with the chartreuse polka dots? Don't tell me you can't find it. I ironed it and hung it on the door knob in clear view!'

...when he gets a new power tool.
He is happy for a week, whistling and
humming to himself as he cuts and saws and
drills holes in every inch of the house. Too bad
we live on a boat.

I find his socks and sweaty underwear all rolled up under the far reaches of our bed. We both work and can't keep a dog or a cat, so these wonderfully round, soft, warm, fuzzy creatures make me feel so cosy. I've even taken to naming them - Roquefort, Penicillin and Streptococci - 'Cocky' for short.

...when he shows how masculine he is and shows off his scar in public. It's a nasty four-inch slice right across his stomach. Got it playing sports. He was goalie. Twenty-seven stitches. Table football can be rough.

...when he watches sports on TV. That's because of the new house rule: when the game is on he has to give me a back rub. Now I'm the one suggesting we watch TV sports: bowling, darts, croquet - tiddly winks championship anyone?

...when we spend all night snuggling on the couch together. Then he delicately reaches across my chest, nibbles my ear and fondles the remote control.

...when he is the expert on everything. He always has the right answer, the last word and a perfect memory. He is never wrong, according to him. He always has an opinion and, coincidentally, it is also the truth. It's like being married to God, without the nuisance of having to keep everything spotless and pure.

...when he grinds the car gears when shifting. And then he looks at me and wonders how I made him do that.

...when he decides that the family should go camping for the weekend. Fortunately for me it takes him two full days to pack the gear and he can never find all the tent stakes. We've actually only used the equipment once, that was when he first bought it and we tried it out in the back garden. (Note: tent stakes are great for crocheting, cooking potatoes and propping up windows).

...when he calls up his buddies for a cookout on a rainy day. As it turns, out you don't need lighter fluid with a gas grill. But his eyebrows have almost grown back and everybody had a good laugh.

...when he uses his Computer Loco-map Quest System. He was able to print out a full-colour, all-country directional locator map to find my mother's house. Never mind that she lives in the flat above us.

He calls me his 'little Ferrari' in bed. Then he pretends he is 'Speed Racer', pops that baby into gear and does 0-60 in ten seconds. Next time, I suggested, he needs to spend more time polishing the chrome if he wants to improve his performance around the track.

...when he gives me what I ask for. I asked for a bidet in the bathroom and just last night he left the toilet seat up, so I got to sit right down in a bowl of ice cold water for a full fifteen minutes before I could reach the towel bar and hoist myself out.

...when he brags about beating the car salesman down £5,000 on the list price, and then adds a CD player, bigger speakers, a moon roof, hydraulic wheels, night vision, cruise control, voice-activated mobile phone, and deluxe cup holder.

...when he can stand still for two hours watching a forklift and front-end loader at a construction site. The last time he stood that still was on our wedding day, but I eventually dislodged him and got him up to the altar.

...when he works hard. But now he is staying late every night working with his new Personal Digital Assistant. I wonder if she is a blonde?

...when he comes home with a
scheme to make millions overnight.
I must be the only woman in the country
with enough knives, herbal algae bath salts,
vitamins, cleaning supplies, phone cards,
powdered protein, encyclopedias and
solar-powered address books to
last until Y3K.

...when he takes me out to the ballet. Even if his favourite part is, as he says, 'half-time'. I appreciate the effort he makes, even if I do have to roll him over and put two pillows under his head to stop the snoring.

...when he does his workout at home. Good thing I insisted that he buy the equipment in solid chrome. Now the Nordickgym, the Bummobile, and The Abs-Normal Rower all sit in the foyer doubling as coat rack, hat stand and shoe caddy.

...when he cooks dinner for me.
I had forgotten just how many pots and pans
and dishes I owned until I saw them in the
sink all at once this morning.

...when he whips out his intergalactic *GPS Global Do-Hickey* to locate the Tower of London. And it's so reassuring to know that if it moves we will be the first ones on the block to be able to find it.

...when he vows he never cries at stupid, mushy, romantic chick flicks. But he always has an allergic reaction at the sad parts, blowing his nose, coughing and wiping watering eyes. It's probably due to bad ventilation in the cinema.

...when he remembers my birthday.
He told me that the new chrome spoke wheels
for the family van would give me the respect I
needed out on the motorway and that
spells S.A.F.E.T.Y.!

...when the toilet overflows and he rises to the occasion. He grabs the wrench and saw, before heading to the basement to fix the problem. Last time he was there for the afternoon and the water got so deep in the basement the coastguard put up small craft warnings.

He goes to the hardware shop for a
box of nails and picture-hanging wire
and returns with a variable-abrasive-saber-
rip-saw-table drill. For the price of a second
car we now have a home filled with birdhouses
and stackable tray tables. Something I love
to remember as I carry the shopping
home in my bicycle basket
after work.

...when he tells the same story over and over again at parties. But the best part is he exaggerates so much each time it's like hearing a completely new story!

...when he pretends that he hasn't been sneaking tastes of the party food beforehand. As if I wouldn't notice that the cake for my Gran now says, 'Happy Birth'. I thought I had cured him when he went about sneaking pâté in the plastic container and it was dog food. But then he said it wasn't bad on the crackers shaped like little bones.

...when he invites his mother to stay for two weeks. Which just happens to coincide with his annual sales convention in Norfolk. The total time he sees her: twenty minutes at the train station as their connections overlap. The total time I am to entertain her: fourteen days plus the rest of her life.

...when he invests for our future by hoarding vast amounts of collectibles. He now has every copy of *Sports Illustrated*, *PC World* and *Popular Mechanic* since 1966. They are particularly valuable because they have never been read.

...when he tells me over and over that size is not important. But then he has to buy the longest boat, biggest car, loudest speakers, most powerful computer and smokes a cigar the size of a cricket bat. I don't get it - maybe I'm mathematically challenged?

...when he buys me sexy lingerie from Sedrick's of Follywood. The problem is it has so many straps and such little material that I feel like I'm getting into a badminton net with the feathered birdies covering my boobies.

...when he does the laundry for me. Eat your heart out Calvin Klein. Thanks to him we are now retro and tie-dyed. Who would have thought that two orange crayons, a red magic marker and one fountain pen could cover so much fabric?

...when he buys something expensive for the house as a surprise. Last week it was a room-sized, black velvet painting of Jesus at the Last Supper, portrayed by Elvis on a Harley. And I am sure there is no connection between that and my mother's recent relapse.